David McCooey

The Book
of Falling

UPSWELL

First published in Australia in 2023
by Upswell Publishing
Perth, Western Australia
upswellpublishing.com

ISBN: 978-0-6455369-7-3

A catalogue record for this
book is available from the
National Library of Australia

Cover design by Chil3, Fremantle
Typeset in Foundry Origin by Lasertype

Upswell Publishing is assisted by the State of Western Australia
through its funding program for arts and culture.

Department of
**Local Government, Sport
and Cultural Industries**
GOVERNMENT OF
WESTERN AUSTRALIA

Endorsements for *The Book of Falling*

The Book of Falling might be the best poetic response to this subject since *Paradise Lost*, but David McCooey's range is greater than Milton's. He's also briefer, sharper, and funnier. Whether raising a sceptical eyebrow at the modern world, picking through the trappings of his childhood, or simply enjoying being alive (after he almost wasn't), McCooey offers us ways of seeing that are immediately clear, yet utterly strange. We smile— and occasionally laugh out loud—at his vivid aperçus, yet we sense the poet's vulnerability and a sort of buried pain. *The Book of Falling* brings us McCooey at the height of his powers, his technique so assured that all seems effortless and inevitable. And there's a surprise in nearly every line.

ANDREW FORD, COMPOSER, BROADCASTER, WRITER

After reading *The Book of Falling*, I felt shaken, brought down to earth, and held. McCooey has that rare knack for genuinely revelatory images and metaphors. Seemingly disparate experiences and objects resonate with fresh energy. Here, he examines the homely and the unhomely, the burden and plasticity of language, the gravity of history crashing into the present—and is examined in turn. This is a capacious book of elegies and meditations, both exacting and vulnerable, remembering parents, animals, words, the living world as we know it.

ANDY JACKSON, POET

The Book of Falling renders instances of human falling, and failing—on domestic and global scales; in the contours of private and public histories, alternate histories and their attendant futures—with compassion and humour. McCooey traverses the 'close geographies' of nostalgia and grief, and the absurd forms of the present, through the finely tuned interplay of elegy and satire, text and image.

BELLA LI, POET

David McCooey

David McCooey was born in England to Scottish and Welsh parents, and came to Australia when he was three years old. He is the author of four previous collections of poetry, including *Blister Pack* (Salt, 2005), which won the Mary Gilmore Award and was shortlisted for four other major literary awards, *Outside* (Salt 2010), which was shortlisted for the Queensland Literary Awards, and *Star Struck* (UWAP, 2016). His poetry appeared in ten of the last eleven editions of *The Best Australian Poems* series, and it has been widely anthologised nationally and internationally. McCooey has appeared at numerous major literary festivals, and his work has been broadcast on ABC Radio National. McCooey is the deputy general editor of the prize-winning *Macquarie PEN Anthology of Australian Literature* (2009). He is the author of a prize-winning monograph on Australian autobiography, and numerous essays and reviews in various books, journals, and newspapers. He is also a sound artist and composer. *The Apartment* (in collaboration with Paul Hetherington, 2018) is his most recent album.

Also by David McCooey:

Poetry
Star Struck
Outside
Graphic
Blister Pack

Audio
The Apartment (with Paul Hetherington)
The Double
Outside Broadcast

Criticism
The Limits of Life Writing (co-editor)
Artful Histories: Modern Australian Autobiography

Anthology
Macquarie PEN Anthology of Australian Literature (deputy general editor)

When I fall into the abyss, I go straight into
it, head down and heels up, and I'm even
pleased that I'm falling in just such a humiliating
position, and for me I find it beautiful.
And so in that very shame I suddenly begin a hymn.

Fyodor Dostoevsky, *The Brothers Karamazov*

'Ha!' The chief laughed again. 'Only one
story and what would that be?'
'The fall from grace.'

Megan Dunn, *Tinderbox*

Lives I

Questions of Travel

Elizabeth Bishop packs for Seattle, December 1965

'Thus, liminality is frequently likened to death, to being in the womb,
to invisibility, to darkness, to bisexuality, to the wilderness, and to
an eclipse of the sun or moon.' Victor Turner, *The Ritual Process:
Structure and Anti-Structure* (1969).

The unseen night creatures—scaled and feathered
for their occult ceremonies—rasp and call outside
in the dark beyond the half dark that
surrounds this marbled, half-lit house.
There is little to occupy my nest of suitcases
on the narrow bed: the hillock of a portable typewriter,
a few pairs of shoes, three suits,
a middle-aged woman's underclothes,
a clutch of diaries and letters,
The Poetics of Music (Vintage Books, 95¢).
Some other books will go by sea,
boxed in a ship's vast and steely womb,
or else be left to visitors and the foxing elements.
There is, after all, nothing too large or too small
that can't be left to the *mise-en-scène* of Brazil,
framed in this teeming window.

This house, midway between city and jungle,
is not indifferent to politics and promenades,
carnivorous plants and tidal rivers.
Neighbouring houses, though, are lit with gasoline,
and tenanted by defeated goats and unbrushed horses.
Underneath us all, the heavy, red earth keeps faith
with the human structures built upon it,
as if there was no such thing as
hubris or landslides or phone lines.
Meanwhile living things spring and decline,
in their godless and Biblical manner.

Obscene and prodigious vegetables are revered here.
Leather-skinned men work their Virgilian work
and hang their homely pots of lunch
on the shaded branches of trees.
The region's fog, the rain and rainbows,
the obdurate sun; they were only ever
metaphors for the weather we call emotion,
that daily melodrama of violence and rectitude,
like an updating of all the old hymns.

The moon now set, I will sleep alone
like Sappho, leaving only the mirror to report—
in its contrary way—on the state of things.
Tomorrow begins the condition we call 'in transit'
(Rio—Lima—Miami—Los Angeles—Seattle);
all those hours to think upon a decade
of time spent in the close geographies
of vehicles, gardens, and rooms.

All these human thresholds will one day give way
to a place beyond cities and hills, plains and jungles—
to a splendid and heartless *book*,
where it is neither night nor day,
neither here nor there, neither me nor you;
a place where a rain endlessly pours,
with nothing ever to break its fall.

Fleeting

Sylvia Plath at 80.

I have outstayed the old millennium,
lost count of years, and jobs, and meals prepared.
My children have careers; the students of my students teach.
    I have had some fame, though
    a little is enough, I know.

In an earlier age, my youthful world conspired
to render me with fires of grief,
at which I bent, and murmured my beginner's German.
And then came, as if I'd called them up,
    the mess of childbirth,
    the bedlam of men and women.

I wrote those poems—the ones for which I'm known—
in the coldest winter for two hundred years.
The snowfalls stretched telephone wires to the ground.

The children and I hid from the historic cold
as if hiding from a fairy-tale monster.
The monster froze the river, ground, and air,
while I outstared, through all those monochrome days,
    the gaze of that greater madness
    I'd called my calling.

Then my discovery: the deranging noise—
like bees or the airy sea—that filled my stony head
was merely fleeting, like snow, or flowers, or husbands' lies
    on crackling telephone lines.
Or the brief duration of abysmal sleep.

Marilyn Monroe Divines the Future

I see omens in the splintering light:
funereal headlines in the newspaper dawn;
the blue glow of touch screens;
the night sky's indifferent radiance;
piercing beams in a thousand movie theatres.

I see hash tags, conspiracies, limited
television series, aliens, and filibusters.
I see my own face endlessly repeated,
triptychs—all the usual paraphernalia
of iconography, glorious and tawdry.

I see *Of Women and Their Elegance*,
I see the fake viral Marilyn Monroe quotes
on Instagram. I see my letters sold
in auction houses, and my old copy of
The Brothers Karamazov.

I see library catalogues and their subjects:
'Marilyn Monroe—Relations with Men'.
I see TV signals in space of me singing
'Happy Birthday, Mr President',
my dress like starlight on snow.

I see Mr President shot dead,
and his widow's majestic grief.
I see children—some almost infants—
shot down like presidents, and presidents
helpless in their great office of power.

I see abusers and those abused,
and I see stories in the news,
official reports, and those
who vehemently deny those reports.
But I say yes: me too, me too.

I see the Queen of England, my age exactly,
whose hand I once shook.
I see so far into the future, you wouldn't comprehend.
I see who will be forgotten first:
Queen Elizabeth, Molly Bloom, or me.

I see my sister, who married a man
named Paris Miracle. I see her in old age,
remembering the linden trees of Kentucky,
the underside of the leaves
flickering white in the plain American sun.

Human & non-human

Anthropocene

Even now, at this late hour,
there is a world entirely free
of names. No days of the week.

No anniversaries or hours, even
when the air is free of light,
or rife with backlit insects.

No epochs, not even that
augural one we have named
after ourselves.

Words span the globe.
Islands of garbage.
Bags of oily waste.

Elegy

Endless cloudwork.

    Ragged mountains, and the ruins

        of astonished volcanoes.

            The promise of oceans.

        Billions of leaves,

      casually dropped over millions of years.

Honey and maggots.

      Stoical lakes.

        Cacophony of insects.

           Smoke and mist.

        Birdlife: the poised and the frantic.

      Wily cephalopods and platonic jellyfish.

The four-legged creatures,

      raising their heads

           to take in landscape.

                  Forests finding their limits.

           The severe night sky

      with its singular moon.

Uncountable orphaned stars.

Blue Hour

After the heat, we open the heavy glass door,
and listen to the stereophonic evening:

spectral traffic; a barking dog; insect drone.
One insect, whirring like a windup paper toy,

has been caught by some larger creature.
The insect clicks loudly, like an ancient sprinkler,

until it makes no noise at all.
Meanwhile the bats in the ironbark tree

are taking to the sky. Their breathtaking wings
have an extensive repertoire of sounds:

a fire igniting; wind-in-the-grass; the beating
of drums; and bats in a horror movie.

And now rain has started to fall, half-heartedly,
as if we were in some other country,

Japan or Korea, perhaps. And our neighbours,
our human neighbours, are—as ever—oddly silent.

Rain poem

And as if someone uttered the trigger word,
rain begins without ceremony.

But it's not 'driving rain';
it's just sitting outside,

engine idling over the neighbourhood.
It's neither coming nor going.

It doesn't give a damn.
And then, like a poem ending,

you look out the window,
and the rain has stopped,

the birds have returned, and the wind
has begun its invisible cover-up job.

Animal Studies

Old man on his mobile phone:
'How's the rabbit going?'

*

The tuna's tune
is its aroma.

*

Charlie and I
walk together
in the weather;

me in my coat,
the dog in his jacket.

*

Why do we keep
falling for the myth
of the micro pig?

*

Humble bee,
laden with pollen
and symbology.

*

A conservative firebrand
raps on tv wearing
a pink-and-purple
bear costume.

Dreams

Your id doesn't give a fuck
about cultural appropriation
or what is appropriate
in the workplace.

It takes you half the morning
to shake off the memory
of that improper kiss,
or the leisurely, slow-mo

sense of falling.
Dreams are slow
not Taylor Swift.
They will not let you go,

when all you want is
to make it out the house,
into the actual morning,
populated by innocent birds,

the neutral sound of traffic,
and the insane barking
of the neighbour's dog,
which must be hounded

by unknown wordless dreams
of freedom or (more likely)
the recall of canine pack hierarchy,
where everything's as it seems.

Slater

At a touch,
the *Star Wars* troop carrier
transforms into an
aardvark football.

Onset of a Theme

The night-time wind sweeps its baton among the rubbish behind some anonymous buildings. Dust and paper; daytime junk—the wind lifts them up. *Scherzo* (meaning joke); *bagatelle* for plastic bags. The moon looks on, unmanned spotlight from high up in the gods.

'What the hell,' says the wind, out of breath and old already. Tired of personification, it settles into nothingness and absence. The security camera, unmoved, caught none of it. But a grey cat, crouched beneath a German SUV, blinks its eyes as if tapping out a secret message. Inconsequential or of immense import—who's to say?

After the Argument

A feeling of well-being,
recovered in your parked car,
alone in mid-winter.
The vehicle is gently rocked
by a heavy wind,
                    while you sit,
in the sunlit space
of the hothouse windows—
the expanse in the windshield
anonymous and benign,
screening the ravenous birdlife,
gentled by distance.

When you begin to count
the minutes, you start the car
and head back home,
the facts having loosed
their irrational hold on things.

Nocturne

i)
Defeated, cruciform;
his shirt on the bedroom floor
at the end of the day.

ii)
On the bedside table, his glasses case,
accidentally placed upside down—
a giant black beetle
stuck on its back.

iii)
Next to the case
lies the obsidian phone,
full of messages from the air.

iv)
Beyond the room's
uncurtained windows—
a field of silent cattle.

v)
The thin pale pyjamas, folded on the bed,
bring to mind the thin blue Aerogrammes
his mother used to receive—
oh, ages ago.

vi)
She would carefully cut their sealed edges,
a blunt paper knife in her fragile hands.

vii)
One night, he watched her reading,
wholly unmindful of his presence.
The frames of her glasses were
the colour of some nameless insect or plant.

viii)
He turns over his glasses case,
and turns off his phone
(sees his face in the black screen).

ix)
Outside, the solemn cows
shift their weight to the ground,
tucking in their frangible legs.

The Birds

'Intra-acting birds seemed to possess an agency of their own; they suddenly appeared out of nowhere and acted in a peculiar way that demanded interpretation.'

Joakim Goldhahn, *Birds in the Bronze Age* (2019).

One day, after the fires,
birds started attacking our house.

Not like in the old movie,
appearing in their hundreds

and killing innocent townsfolk.
Of course not; these were

just a couple of birds,
appearing every day to

smash their beaks against
our windows, as if to say

Knock, knock. Who's there?
We are small and persistent,

filled with unconscious will.
Only your slomo gigantic bodies

and unlovely voices
will scare us away,

but only for a while, until we
return, shitting where we do,

and attacking the hard
competitors that look

just like us, and which,
like us, never go away.

And so my wife hangs up
imitation owls,

blinding streamers,
and short-lived bells.

She scours the far horizons
of the internet for solutions,

none of which are
entirely effective.

Sometimes she even wishes
for a small rifle,

like the kind her bird-loving father
used to have, shooting,

without remorse,
the fruit-thieving birds

on his property, until the gun laws
changed, and he resorted to nets.

Meanwhile, my wife's friend dreams
about the birds attacking our house.

What does it mean? she wonders,
sending a book of poems—

divinations that give no answers
(though sixteen centuries ago

the king of Alasia put great store in the
tidings of an eagle diviner from Egypt).

Inside our house, glass avian
artwork from Scandinavia

reminds us that we love
what we kill, or dream of killing.

It's surely obvious,
just like in Hitchcock's film,

what the birds have to tell us—
beating their beaks until they bleed,

leaving their pitiful message
higgledy-piggledy on our estate.

Black Summer

We spend the days looking at the sky.
The dogs are all inside.
Somewhere kids are playing 'would you rather'.
Endless newsfeeds never satisfy.
All the anchors are solemn.
The government has nothing to say
about the consequential smoke.

Chamber Pieces

i)

My bedroom is darkened.
My mother steps in soundlessly
to tell me the news about my dog.
It has been put to sleep
for worrying the neighbour's sheep.
What does worrying mean?
It means the dog mauled
the farmer's livestock.
So the farmer testifies.

But it is not my dog; it is my brother's.
And he, like my mother now, is nowhere
to be seen. He is in his silent bedroom
worrying over his loss.

ii)

We are at the dining table.
The window looks out onto bush.

Someone remarks on the view.
'What is a view?' I ask.

My father gestures with his hands.
I look outside at the unfamiliar trees.

iii)

The classroom smells of chalk.
Even then, it has the odour of the past.
It always seems dark inside, the high windows
above us blown out by the colonial light.

I don't question—why would I?—
the reason I spend my days here.
I worry instead that a question
will come my way,
unexpected, full of alien words.

I am unaware that I will spend
my stock of time sitting at desks in the
restrained privilege of quiet rooms.

Opening Titles

A man walks down the hill.
It is the blue hour, and he can see
into the radiant windows
of his neighbours' houses.
A woman bends her head in prayer
at the kitchen sink; a titanic screen
is frantic with men playing sport;
a child jumps on a leather couch.
The *mise-en-scène* is offset
by pink-tinged Rococo cloudwork.
A piano sonata by Haydn—
a movement marked 'Adagio'—
plays as the man descends the hill.
Does it matter if he cannot hear
the music in the remnant light?
He crosses the street, empty of everything,
save for a black cat, which, seeing the man,
posts itself into the black slot
of a stormwater drain.

//

Now the man has reached his house.
He shuts the door against his neighbours
and is himself now inside a golden light.
Night has suddenly fallen,
and the dialogue may commence.

Three photo poems

Posing Cards

Have Mom and Dad stand together
and ask Dad to put his hands in his pockets.

Tell Mom to turn toward Dad
and 'hug' his arm.

Have the couple half hug
with their arms crossing in the front.

If they seem uncomfortable,
ask them to make silly faces

at each other
to loosen them up.

Bring in the youngest child.
Try to use them to fill any empty spaces
between older family members.

Place Mom and Dad
in the standard Mom and Dad sitting pose.

Then bring in the children.

While walking away,
have Mom and Dad stop

and kiss over the child
between them.

Redundancies

The work we do matters.

Thank you again
for the level of care
and support you have shown
during this challenging time.

Our kindness,
and extraordinary commitment,
speaks to who we are
and the values we uphold.

The continued commitment
that you demonstrate
is remarkable.

With any number of
significant activities
on the horizon,
and the ongoing
adaptation and innovation,
our individual and
collective achievements
are tremendous.

Thank you.

Thank you for continuing
to do all you can
to support one another.

I want to assure you that we
are working hard
to provide as much certainty
to you as possible.

I have noted the genuine
warmth and compassion
people show to one another.

I have said before that the fabric
of our community has been woven
with the individual and collective
contributions of thousands of passionate,
committed and capable people.

It is also true that kindness and empathy
are the threads that hold us together.

The road ahead is not clear,
and we still have significant
challenges to face.

Amongst these challenges
we will have new opportunities;
we can shine and define our future.

Our capacity to thrive and shine
will depend on us
continuing to work together.

We will be with you
every step of the way.

Bathroom abstraction

1.

You once wrote the following in an essay: 'His poetry, ambivalent as a bathroom, acknowledges both the body's pleasures and its incompetencies'. In response, a critic wrote that he only *kind of* knew what you meant.

You were talking about the poetry of John Forbes, who died of a heart attack in 1998. In his poem, 'Ode to Tropical Skiing', taking a bath is described as 'a total fucking gas'.

2.

You think about the bathrooms you have encountered since writing that essay almost two decades ago. In particular, the bathrooms of hospitals. Helping your wife, almost unable to stand, wash herself. Outside a nurse asking if she can help, while the baby, helpless in a plastic cot, cries from hunger.

You think about the bathroom you made your way to after your bypass operation. Crossing your hands over your chest and applying pressure, like the nursing staff told you.

3.

Windowless bathrooms are the caves of modernity. In a hotel in Patagonia—a town where the wire fences were covered with scraps of rubbish, frantic in the wind—you find yourself in a suite with a windowless bathroom.

All that space outside, ambiguously beautiful, and still nowhere to let the light in. On the second day, you change rooms.

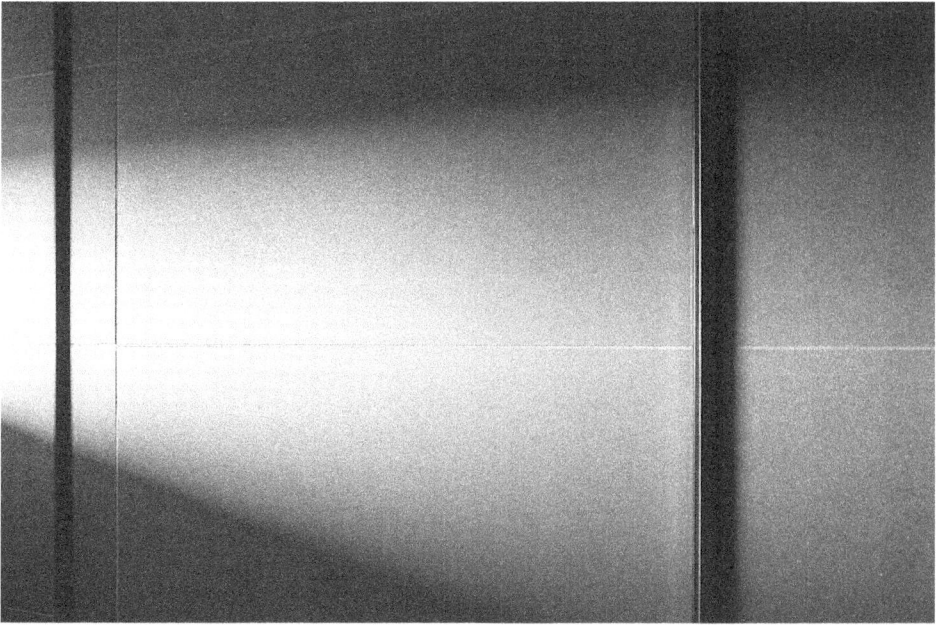

4.

Every day, at home, you are in and out of the bathroom, taking in its fine abstractions, while—utterly human—you shit, and wash, and brush your teeth.

You revel in the gaseous miracle of hot showers. The water, the fatty acids, the skin and hair—it all runs away. The bathroom window frames the outside world, which is simplified by steam and distance.

Satires & elegies

You have been unsubscribed

We tried the whole swearing-at-work thing
but it didn't work out. One of the creatives
asked me to shoot some video of Trent
roasting coffee beans. Afterwards, we stood
in our tuxedoes of silence. On Monday,
I dreamed of the bokeh afforded
by Tokyo neon, while *Le Monde* worried over
neocons in Washington in inscrutable French.
That night, Bella turned to me and said
'Remember when we used to touch
our televisions?' I smiled and returned
to my device, mis-reading 'degenerates'
for 'delegates'; all those Cold-War words
still with us. Meanwhile, I know who
my One Direction soul mate is.

Your Life as a Movie

1. Financing

The relevant parties came
to an agreement.

It was probably best
you weren't around
to witness the pitch.

2. Casting

As a lead, you have no
experience whatsoever,
but here you are.

The supporting cast
are believable enough.
But how often they
struggle to hit their marks
and remember their lines.

3. Filming

There was every kind
of weather, and the
money was often
touch and go.

Every shot was
a one-take, but
additional photography
continues to this day.

4. Editing

Long shots, long shots,
always with the long shots.
But the montage
sequences hold up okay.

Every night, in the editing suite
of your bedroom, you
unpick the day's rough cut.
…………………………………
…………………………………

5. Underscoring

The composer has supplied
only the most basic of scores—
it could be your heartbeat.
Barely audible on the
soundtrack of your life,
it will come to a dramatic end
just as the credits start to roll.
Listen out for it.

Extracts from an Interview

Q. Where do you get your ideas?
Jesus wept, my father used to say.
What you hear when the fridge stops making a noise.
Books and other forms of ESP.
Bats in the ironbark tree.
The light from torches, which children find compelling.
Breaking and entering.
My better half; my better nature.
The internet, of course.
Animals, vehicles, buildings, faces, music, books.
All those things in movies.
Memories that want to be scratched like cats.
Cats, insouciant and fearful.
The night the night the night—

Q. How do you feel about critics?
After the downpour,
my son puts on an LP:
Neil Young's *On the Beach*.

Q. What was your first experience of a literary festival?
My first taste of fame (someone else's, of course) was when, in my
mid-twenties, I shared a stage with a writer whose book was the
biggest book of the year in the English-speaking world. It was a
misery memoir; not that we used that term in those days. When I
say 'shared the stage', I mean I was the moderator. I introduced him
and fielded the questions from the audience. In my introduction I got
a big laugh from quoting a reader's review on Amazon.com (a new
thing then). The review was something along the lines of 'I want to
have your children'. The writer smiled affably at that. He stood up
to talk, clutching the lectern like a politician, sending forth the pork
barrelling of his phraseology.

Q. What quality do you most admire in a writer?
Brevity, concision, and the avoidance of redundancy.

Australia

Dropping my son at school.
It is 'Art Day';
students are to dress up
as their favourite artist.

I see a kid dressed in white.
He has sunscreen on his nose,
and carries a cricket bat.

America / Japan

The people are so friendly, but it's hard to know what they really think.

They like baseball!

They have traditional food, and they eat burgers and pizza.

Their cities are so big.

It is a nation of contradictions.

They believe in hard work.

The record stores are amazing; a whole wall of noise cassettes.

Their women are not subservient, but spirited and steadfast.

Eating Money

Convert your currency into American dollars; cotton and linen are easy to digest. Don't force too many bills into your mouth at once. Try cutting them up into smaller pieces. You might like to scatter these pieces over a salad, or use them in place of parsley when garnishing a meal. Try keeping a handful in your pocket to snack on when you're at home or out and about. They are a great way of getting your greens, and good for the circulation.

Be careful with coins. You can warm coins in your hand, or put them in your mouth like a stone. But you cannot swallow them. Coins are for the poor.

Ubi Sunt

Where are Dave Dee, Dozy, Beaky, Mick & Tich?
What happened to smelling salts?
What happened to the information superhighway?
What happened to caps on CEOs' incomes?
What happened to Julie Christie and Hayley Mills?
What happened to ministers taking responsibility?
What happened to *Where Are They Now*?
Whither the novel?
What happened to booting up and mainframes?
What happened to wealth redistribution?
Where are the snows of yesteryear?
Where are the four trillion metric tons of Antarctic ice?
Where is Bennett's Seaweed and the Daintree Banana?
Where is the Tasman Starling, the Lord Howe Pigeon, and the
    Tasmanian Emu?
Where is the Broad-Faced Potoroo and the Dusky Flying Fox?
Where is the Thylacine?
Where are the princes of the nations, and those who rule over the
    beasts on earth?
Where are those who hoard up silver and gold, for whom there is no
    end to their getting?
They have vanished and others have taken their place.

Television: An Elegy

i)
Space junk for a moon landing,
its cold lunar light
blue-rinsed a billion chambers.

Our radio-age parents
were held in its dazzle,
even as they repurposed
for their children
that old zombie-theory
from the Age of the Novel.

ii)
We thought TVs were everywhere,
but bars, waiting rooms, and airports
were all innocent of their presence.
The news crawl was a thing of the future.

iii)
TV was an almost-portal
for the vacant times:
after-school; endless Sundays;
up-too-late.

It squatted on our lives,
first teacher of desire,
parsed as eros and violence.
It inaugurated us
into the ritual of the jump scare,
and proved that spectacle
is simultaneity:
Wimbledon; Evel Knievel;

the wonderment of royalty;
reports of assassinations.
Disaster upon disaster,
like flaming logs
collapsing in the fireplace.

Vestiges of the 1970s

The glamour of submarines
with improved acoustic stealth.

*

Cryogenics for
ghastly billionaires.

*

Robots getting
their act together.
(Any day now.)

*

Actual and rhetorical
threats against democracy.

*

Talk of sports and
decriminalising abortion.

*

Global warming,
and the glamorous
houses of the future.

*

Shock-jocks,
professional creeps,
on AM radio.

*

Visions of countless solar panels
in a vast, tangerine desert.

*

Honourable members spruiking
Australia as a rice-growing
capital of the world.

Moog Elegy

i)
Those in the know
knew that the
medial digraph
of the name 'Moog'
was in fact
a diphthong:

a vocative 'O',
not a vulgar 'oo'.

ii)
The particular magic
of Moog's inventions,

we are often told,
was in the filters—

in the way they
sculpted a waveform.

It was, in other words,
the old-fashioned magic

of giving and taking
away at the same time.

Schooling in the '70s

For years they plagued us
with 'Morning Has Broken'.

But we were fortunate:
corporal punishment,

like global war and uniforms,
had been done away with.

Each day we went home to
hand-me-down tv shows

from the 1960s, already vintage.
In 1975, my teacher told

the class that Whitlam
should be given a chance.

I reported this over dinner,
and my parents were incensed.

Each week we sang
'God Save the Queen'.

We weren't allowed
the Sex Pistols,

but sex education
was our birthright.

The world was going
to change so much.

Anagrammatic

Memory

Me,
or
my.

*

My autobiography

Buy
atrophy,
amigo.

*

Occupations

Cap on
coitus.

*

Identity

Tiny
diet.

Last four lines

I was the romcom auteur,
the unspoken presence
at your birthday party,
brittle drink in your glass.

Late Capitalism

In a tourist town in
New Zealand,
a restaurant
called 'Hell'
sports a sign
neatly taped to its window:
'Part Time Staff Wanted'.

Drop Tower

Was this the dream they were promised at the gates
where the father paid the entrance fee?
The daughter cleared the ride's height requirement
and they were strapped in, with strangers.
Their legs dangled from the gondola
like the limbs of the unconscious.
They rose, a tourist-apotheosis into the empty sky,
where they took in the consoling view,
like the condemned were once sometimes allowed.
The distant hills gave a suggestion
of the sublime highs and lows of real-estate.
And then they fell,
                    as if from a skyscraper.

Seconds later,
the ride finished as the rare-earth magnets kicked in,
and they were softly gathered to the ground
in some fantastic but real feat of physics.
They left the area, astounded by gravity.
And then they saw the on-ride photos for sale:
low-res snaps of witnesses to an atrocity;
the smeared dark O of the daughter's mouth.
Later, strapped in their car, and heading towards
the freeway, they could hear the screams.

RIP

Ubiquity unveils the zeitgeist.
'Rest in peace' becomes 'Rest in power'.

The young, like their devices,
are everywhere, too,

discovering new words like
'precariat', 'misgender', and 'fatberg',

while I delete account after account.
I don't even have the ballyhoo

to upload a jpeg anymore.
I'm not concerned about the deep state.

I am concerned about all states:
states of undress, states of mind.

I try my best to ignore
the state of being at rest—

in that eternal kind of way, I mean.
But if I was, would I be hoping

for peace or for power?
It has to be one or the other,

because unlike Truth and Beauty
you can't have both together.

History

Children pick stones to throw across the border.

Dry goods change hands over dirty counters.

An open door reveals darkness fleeing down a hallway.

A black-handled knife cuts the bloodless meat.

Gloves divine the violent fidelity of rope.

The applauding crowd reveals itself.

Revolutions

A month after the royal family was shot
and buried beneath the trees of an unknown forest,
the girl came to stay with us; the connection
was tenuous (an associate of a friend of a cousin),
but the household was on edge,
which was only to be expected.
The day she arrived, I smeared some pig fat in her hair
and put her to work in the kitchen.
'No special favours,' I said to the cook.
Less than a month later, soldiers arrived
under a sky the colour of birch sap.
Three men made their way through the house,
until a dozen bodies stood in the cold,
not daring to stamp or complain.
Eventually, the officer got out of his black car.
The noise of the closing door ricocheted off the house.
Standing before the girl, he tried to
catch her out with French:
'On dit que ta famille est morte.'
They say your family is dead.
The girl looked uncomprehendingly
at the dark square of ground in front of her.
(Schooling her in ignorance had been easy.)
The soldiers spent the rest of the morning
at the house, asking questions, occasionally shouting,
drinking the hot drinks that we offered them.
Eventually the men left, without assurances or threats.
The night she was to be taken to France,
her hair and hands now clean,
I gave her a gift—a small Bible.
She thanked me with a bow of the head,
and stood waiting, book in hand.
The Bible's leather covers were black
like the soil under the bare trees outside.

Grief

Old-fashioned,
it calls unannounced
with worn-out news
that never fails
to surprise.

*

One day it is grand
and dramatic; the next
a small, pathetic thing.

Or rather it turns
days into these.

*

Its pride is to expose
life's last mystery.

Or rather, the next-to-last.

A Brief Family History of Falling

1.
It was a family joke that my father,
while drunk, fell from a diving board

by a swimming pool in Nigeria.
Stepping aside, as if to say 'After you,'

to the intoxicated man behind him,
his good manners led to the concrete below,

a cracked skull, and a broken pelvis.
'Daft bugger,' my mother would say,

laughing at the dinner table, where that story
would sporadically be related.

Only years later did she tell me of the time
she saw him in London after his accident;

it must have been around 1960.
He was a broken man, and she felt sorry for him,

which I took to be her way of saying
that she fell in love with him.

2.
My mother had her own history of falling.
In 1969, she fell on or over a low

brick wall outside our house.
The skin graft on her leg,

and my own anxious non-memory,
were the remnants of that event,

which travelled with us to Australia.
In 1978, on a boat, during a rough

crossing to Rottnest Island,
my mother fell and broke a rib.

Two years earlier, she had fallen in the kitchen,
insisting I call friends—not an ambulance.

Decades later, she fell in the street,
an old woman helped by strangers,

shocked by the blood on the pavement.
Her final fall in 2020 was bloodless and solitary.

3.
My father fell off a ladder in 1983.
I was inside watching *High Noon*.

It was long minutes before I realised
what the noise outside signified.

I found him by the pool; the doctors
found he had broken his pelvis.

He fell off another ladder in 1986,
while avoiding chicken-carving responsibilities.

In 1999, sitting in his car at traffic lights,
a large tree fell, crushing the car

with my father in it. His Christmas that year
was spent in hospital, my mother spooning

roast turkey into his mouth. After his death
in 2013, I unpinned from the wall of his study

a photograph of his destroyed vehicle,
the image cured from years of afternoon sun.

Synaptic Transmissions: An Elegy

'The remembrance of things past does require a specialized system involving the medial temporal lobe and the hippocampus.'

Eric R. Kandel, *Journal of Neuroscience* 29.41: 2009.

My father can be in two places at once
(a trick I wish he could not do):
distributed in the silt of Llandrindod Wells Lake,
and in the folds of my brain
(though the second of these places
is merely a figure of speech).

He becomes real in a human sense
in the synaptic transmissions
that might occur a dozen or so
times a day across the globe:
my mother, his sisters, my siblings.

When he had his stroke,
he was at home, his evening meal
(never eaten) about to be served.
He looked at the floor and said
'There is something wrong
with my name.'
And some days later,
his brain function having ceased,
he was officially declared
no longer a person—
the remnant of a person.

Now he is heavy as a thought
distributed in the deep
sediment of my memory,
in the uncanny articulation of a gesture,
a signal from a dying star.

Lives II

Arigato

i

'Thank you very much' in Japanese is *arigato gozaimasu*.

ii

M remembered the phrase by linking '*arigato*' with 'alligator'. One evening, as M and his wife were walking the streets of Kyoto, he saw a cartoon-like picture of a half-alligator, half-robot creature on the side of a vending machine. '*Arigato gozaimasu*,' M said to himself, walking past the brightly lit machine.

iii

Gozaimasu is a polite and archaic form of 'to be' and, M supposed, with *arigato*, the phrase meant something like 'there is thanks'. But M is no linguist, and he was in a foreign country, so he used the phrase without entirely understanding it.

iv

It was only in looking the phrase up on the internet that he saw the spelling included a terminal, and seemingly unspoken, '*u*'.

v

While in Kyoto, M was proud to learn '*arigato gozaimashita*', which was a formal way of thanking someone once a process had been completed; when one had entered a restaurant, ordered a meal, eaten it, paid for it, and was now finally leaving, for instance. M was taught this by Mazda, one of his guides, who simplified his name (which was Matsuda) for the tourists, and who had studied linguistics at university.

vi

While in Japan, M used and heard the phrase *arigato gozaimasu* so often that there were nights the words repeated over and over in his head as he fell asleep. '*Arigato gozaimasu*,' he murmured to himself as he crossed the threshold to unconsciousness.

vii

But despite saying the phrase, mantra-like, to himself every day, there were times when, inexplicably, he couldn't remember what to say when he had to thank someone (as one does countless times when being a tourist). He would usually remember the '*arigato*' part, but sometimes nothing at all came to him, and he would simply smile and make small bows, in the hope he was making his gratitude apparent.

viii

At one point, sitting in an Italian restaurant called Napoli, he felt the lack of the phrase so intently that he wondered if it was a sign of imminent dementia. 'Your father had a poor memory when he got older,' M's wife suggested helpfully. 'He always had a poor memory,' M said. 'Perhaps that was because he didn't pay enough attention to things,' M's wife said.

ix

'*Arigato gozaimashita*,' M said to his wife or to no-one, once they had paid the bill and were outside the restaurant.

x

Later, M remembered how his father had once told a story about swimming in a crocodile-infested river in Papua New Guinea. His father was in a foreign country and had perhaps not followed, or understood, some unspoken rule.

xi

In Papua New Guinea there are hundreds of languages, and therefore presumably hundreds of ways to give thanks.

Gesang der Jünglinge (Song of the Youths)

Every Christmas, M's mother would play war-time Bing Crosby. His father would counter with the Choir of King's College, Cambridge. The boy choristers were school children, like M. But M's class only sang carols every summer at the old people's home down the road. Most of their audience looked like they had given up eating.

In high school—Christmas carols behind him—M bought so many LP records that he would sneak them into his bedroom. One day, he arrived home with Karlheinz Stockhausen's *Gesang der Jünglinge*, with its mix of electronic sound and a recording of a boy soprano shuffled around the stereo field. Stockhausen had planned to write a mass, but he was told that loudspeakers had no place in a church. On this day, M's father caught him before he could reach his bedroom, asking to see what M had bought. M sheepishly slipped the record out of its paper bag and showed his father. 'I don't give you pocket money to buy Stockhausen,' he said. 'But it's Deutsche Grammophon,' M said, pointing to the august yellow label, and M's father laughed.

Years later, M told this story at his father's funeral service. As M spoke, he could hear his father's old friends shuffling their feet on the chapel floor, and his young son—untouched by the fires of memory—calling out for food.

Inside the Whale

M and his son are watching Walt Disney's *Pinocchio*.

//

The wooden boy, Pinocchio, has jumped into the ocean to look for his father, a poor woodcarver, who has been swallowed by Monstro, the whale. 'Father!' calls Pinocchio, his voice pitifully distorted by the water. 'Father!' It is one of the saddest sounds M has ever heard.

//

Meanwhile, Pinocchio's father—who had in turn been searching for Pinocchio—is starving to death in the belly of the whale.

//

For the first couple of years after his father's death, M's sister and mother would call to remind him it was the anniversary of his father's death. 'I don't want to know!' M would say. 'That's just my way of handling it,' he would claim—ashamed, a wilful child who knows he is in the wrong.

//

But Pinocchio is a good little boy. In fact, he frees his father from the whale, at the cost of his own life.

//

Back in the woodcarver's cottage, Pinocchio's inert body has been laid out on his bed. His father is bereft. But a blue fairy brings Pinocchio back to life—now as a real boy—as a reward for his selflessness.

//

'I'm a real boy!' says M's son, mimicking Pinocchio, relieved at the fairy-tale ending. He runs outside to his mother, who is working in the garden. 'I'm a real boy,' he says, as if he has just discovered the fact.

//

Inside, M wonders at the blue fairy, bringing Pinocchio back to life, gifting him mortality anew. (If he wasn't a real boy before, how could he die?)

//

The film is finished; the day is over. While his son talks himself to sleep, M sits by a window looking onto the street, the whole world caught in the giant belly of the night.

Acknowledgments

These poems were written on Wadawurrung country. I acknowledge the traditional custodians of the land on which I live.

'Posing Cards' and 'Redundancies' employ found text. I have employed these (unattributed) words written by others as part of a long-standing tradition of poetic transformation. The photographs in 'Posing Cards' are by my late father, Wyndham McCooey. The photographs in 'Redundancies' and 'Bathroom Abstract' are my own.

A number of poems in this collection appeared (often in a different form) in *Cordite Poetry Review*, *Australian Poetry Journal*, *Meanjin*, *Kenyon Review*, *Rabbit*, *TEXT*, *Stilts*, *Storm Brain: The Hippocrates Book of The Brain*, ed. Wendy French, Michael Hulse, and Donald Singer (2021) and *Shuffle: An Anthology of Microlit*, ed. Cassandra Atherton (2019). My thanks go to the editors of these journals and anthologies for their support. I also offer my thanks to Andrew Ford; 'Black Summer' takes its inspiration from the lyrics I wrote for the song by Andrew that appears in his song cycle, *Red Dirt Hymns* (2020–21). Special thanks, too, for the (often long-standing) support and kindness of my fellow writers, my friends, and the students I have had the privilege to teach and supervise. Many thanks also go to Megan Dunn, and to Andrew Ford, Andy Jackson, and Bella Li for their generous words of support.

Profound thanks go to Terri-ann White.

I must also thank my mother, Phillis McCooey (who passed away during the writing of this book), and my siblings, John McCooey and Phillis Broadhurst, as well as my sister-in-law, Tiina Takolander, and her daughters Charlie Burton and Cassidy Quarrel. Lastly, thank you to my wife, Maria Takolander, and my children, Cate McCooey and Samuel Takolander, 'for everything, not least of all happiness'.

This work is dedicated to the memory of Phillis McCooey (1930–2020).

About Upswell

Upswell Publishing was established in 2021 by Terri-ann White as a not-for-profit press. A perceived gap in the market for distinctive literary works in fiction, poetry and narrative non-fiction was the motivation. In her years as a bookseller, writer and then publisher, Terri-ann has maintained a watch on literary books and the way they insinuate themselves into a cultural space and are then located within our literary and cultural inheritance. She is interested in making books to last: books with the potential to still be noticed, and noted, after decades and thus be ripe to influence new literary histories.

About this typeface

Book designer Becky Chilcott chose
Foundry Origin not only as a strong,
carefully considered, and dependable
typeface, but also to honour her late
friend and mentor, type designer Freda
Sack, who oversaw the project. Designed
by Freda's long-standing colleague,
Stuart de Rozario, much like Upswell
Publishing, Foundry Origin was created
out of the desire to say something new.